Union Public Library
1980 Morris Avenue
Union, N.J. 07083

P9-EMG-213

ALL KINDS OF
FEET

Sara Swan Miller

Union Public Library
1980 Morris Avenue
Union, N.J. 07083

 Marshall Cavendish
Benchmark
New York

Marshall Cavendish Benchmark
99 White Plains Road
Tarrytown, New York 10591-9001
www.marshallcavendish.us

Copyright © 2008 by Marshall Cavendish Corporation

All rights reserved. No part of this book may be reproduced or utilized in any form or by any means elec-
tronic or mechanical, including photocopying, recording, or by any information storage and retrieval
system, without permission from the copyright holders.

All Web sites were available and accurate when this book was sent to press.

Editor: Doug Sanders
Publisher: Michelle Bisson
Art Director: Anahid Hamparian
Series Designer: Alex Ferrari

Library of Congress Cataloging-in-Publication Data

Miller, Sara Swan.
   Feet / by Sara Swan Miller.
       p. cm. — (All kinds of ...)
   Summary: "An exploration of animal feet, their various shapes and
functions"—Provided by publisher.
   Includes bibliographical references (p. 47) and index.
   ISBN-13: 978-0-7614-2520-5
   1. Foot—Juvenile literature. I. Title. II. Series.

   QL950.7.M565 2007
   591.47'9—dc22

                         2006019714

Photo research by Anne Burns Images
Cover photo: Minden Pictures/Pete Oxford

The photographs in this book are used with permission and through the courtesy of: *Corbis:* Markus
Botzek, 1; Stephen Frink, 6; Jeffrey L. Rotman, 10; Theo Allofs, 12; Michael & Patricia Foden, 13, 42; Joe
McDonald, 14, 18; Kevin Schafer, 19; John Conrad, 20; DK Limited, 22; Jim Zuckerman, 23; Jonathan Blair, 24;
Kennan Ward, 28; W. Perry Conway, 32; Jeff Vanuga, 35; Martin Harvey, 36, 38; Tom Brakefield, 39; W. Wayne
Lockwood, M.D., 40. *Animals Animals:* Gerard Lacz, 4; Wild & Natural, 8; Allen Blake Sheldon, 17; Scott W.
Smith, 30; Arthur Morris, 31. *Photo Researchers:* Sheila Terry, 7; R.Andrew Odum, 16. *Peter Arnold:* Tobias
Gremme, 11; Malcolm Schuyl, 43; Klein, 44. *Minden Pictures:* Frans Lanting, 26, 27; Ingo Arndt/Foto Natura,
34.

Printed in Malaysia
1 3 5 6 4 2

CONTENTS

A brook trout has fins instead of legs to help it move about.

GETTING AROUND

Most animals need some way to get from one place to another. How else would they find food, escape from danger, find shelter, and search for mates? Over millions and millions of years, animals have evolved all kinds of ways of getting around. Few animals stay in one place for very long.

Aquatic animals have their own solutions to moving about in their watery world. Some ripple their bodies through the water. Others zoom and dart about with great speed. Some have a sail that lets them glide along the surface. Fish, of course, use fins to balance themselves and steer through the water.

Most land animals, however, along with some aquatic animals as well, developed feet. The ancestors of birds

FISH FINS

The typical fish swims by waving its *caudal fin*, or tail fin, back and forth. A pair of *pectoral fins* behind its head is used for paddling and turning. The *dorsal fin* on its back helps keep the fish stable in the water. A pair of *pelvic fins* on its belly and a single *anal fin* also help keep a fish on an even keel.

A SNAIL'S FOOT

A snail has only one foot. It glides along over a slimy mucus that protects it from sharp objects.

A snail can pull its single foot into its shell.

and flying mammals were originally four-footed land animals. Their front legs evolved into wings that let them soar through the air.

Humans are the only animals that always walk fully erect or straight, not stooped or slumped over. Millions of years ago our ancestors came down from the trees and gradually began walking upright. Our ancient ancestors, Australopithecus, appeared about four million years ago. They had long arms, sloping foreheads, and walked erect. As humans slowly evolved, their brains grew bigger. With their greater intelligence and *opposable thumbs*, they learned to perform all kinds of tasks with their hands. From one line of Australopithecus came another group, *Homo habilis*, which may be our direct ancestor. *Homo habilis* could make tools, carry spears, and hunt and process food in new and inventive ways.

If you look at the human skeleton and muscles, you can see how we are adapted to walk upright. A double curve in our spine takes some of the pressure off the *vertebrae*, which make up the backbone. We also have extra-large muscles in our buttocks that help support our hips, legs, and back.

People, however, have paid a price for walking upright. Despite millions of years of *adaptations*, we can still get backaches from walking around. We have the most trouble in our lower back, because it carries most of the body's weight. We still have some evolving to do before doctors who treat back problems go out of business.

In the rest of the animal world, there is an incredible variety of feet— seemingly endless ways of getting around. Feet come in all shapes and sizes, from tiny mil-lipede legs to the huge flippers of a blue whale. Feet come in different numbers too—one foot, four feet, six feet, eight feet, all the way up to seven hundred feet! Let's find out more about all kinds of feet.

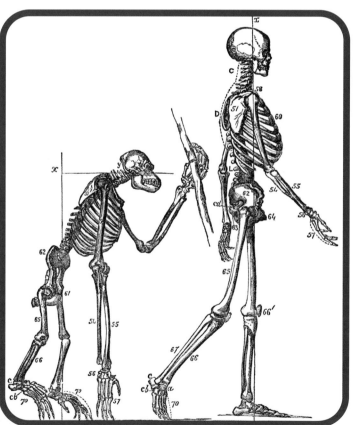

The orangutan skeleton (left) includes a curved back. The human skeleton (right) has a spine with a double curve.

A grasshopper's long, strong hind legs help it bound great distances.

INSECT FEET

Insects are also called hexapods, meaning "six footed." Each of their six jointed legs has five parts, ending with the tarsus. On the end of the tarsus, many insects have a pair of claws that help them grip. Others have pads at the tip that help them hold on to surfaces.

With their light, flexible legs, insects can move very fast. Most of them also have wings. Several, such as a monarch butterfly, can migrate or travel hundreds of miles. Insects' wings are different from birds' wings, however. Birds' wings are actually front limbs that changed through the years into tools for flight. But insect wings are not leg-like. They grow out of an insect's shoulders and are separate from the legs.

There is a great variety of insect legs—each adapted to suit a range of habitats and behavior. Cockroaches, for instance, have long legs that help them run quickly. Grasshoppers have large back legs, perfect for jumping and escaping predators. A grasshopper can jump twenty times its body length. If you had legs like that, you could jump over a house!

Insects that hunt, including praying mantises, often have large forelegs that they can use to grasp and hold

OTHER INVERTEBRATES

How do other invertebrates, or animals without backbones, get around? Some of them do not. Sponges, corals, sea anemones, and barnacles stay anchored in the same place all their adult lives. Other simple invertebrates that have no legs have evolved their own special ways of getting from one place to another. A jellyfish tightens the muscles in its bell-shaped body to push itself forward. A leech moves through the water by changing the shape of its body. A scallop can "fly" through the water by clapping the two halves of its shell together. More complex invertebrates developed legs. Most starfish, for instance, have five arms with suction cups on them. An octopus has eight arms with gripping disks on the underside, and a squid has ten. Lobsters, crabs, and shrimp all have ten jointed legs that they use to creep along the sea bottom. Arachnids—a group that includes spiders, mites, and ticks—all have eight jointed legs.

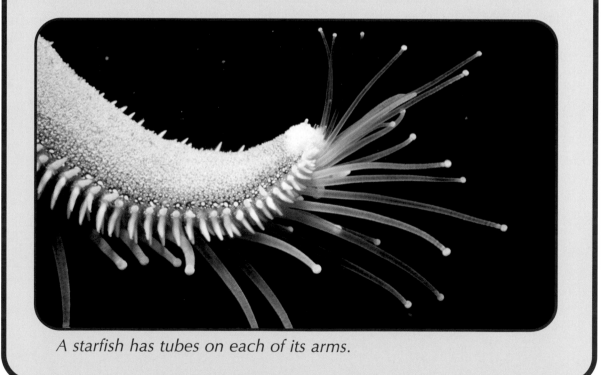

A starfish has tubes on each of its arms.

their prey. A housefly has sticky pads on the ends of its legs that let it walk upside down on the ceiling. A bee also has sticky footpads. As it walks, it folds and unfolds the pads in time with its steps. That keeps the bee from tripping over its own sticky feet. Bees also have pouches made of stiff hairs on their legs where they can pack pollen to take back to the hive.

A praying mantis can grasp its prey with its front claws.

Insects that live in the water have legs specially adapted to their aquatic life. A water strider, for instance, walks along the surface. It has long, thin legs that spread out its weight and keep it from sinking. Whirligig beetles zip around on the surface, pushing themselves along with their paddle-like back feet. Other aquatic insects spend a lot of their time diving underwater in search of food. Their legs are adapted for swimming. Water boat-men, for instance, have flattened middle and hind legs that they use to row about underwater. Hairs on their back legs help them swim even better. These aquatic bugs eat algae and decaying plant material. Their front legs have developed into little scoops that help them collect food.

SPIDER FEET

Like insects' legs, spider legs are adapted to different needs. Web builders have very sensitive feet. They can sense the slightest vibration from an insect caught in their web. Other spiders, such as wolf spiders, are hunters that stalk their prey. Their legs are not as sensitive as web builders', but they are long and powerful. A wolf spider can zip along at quite a rapid rate. Some spiders, including the fishing spider, can skate along on the surface of the water.

Wolf spiders have long legs that help them chase after their prey.

Some insects use their legs for more than getting around. Many have sense organs on their legs. Crickets and katydids, for example, hear through the eardrums on their legs. Most insects have hairs covering their bodies, especially their legs. These hairs can detect chemicals, and thus serve as the insects' sense of smell and taste. Butterflies and flies have especially well-developed smelling and tasting hairs on their feet. Imagine being able to taste with your toes!

HOW MANY FEET?

Some invertebrates have lots of feet. Millipedes may have up to four hundred, and some centipedes have seven hundred!

A giant millipede has hundreds of legs—two pairs on each segment.

*The glass lizard is not a snake,
even though it is sometimes
mistaken for one.*

3

AMPHIBIANS AND REPTILES

What do amphibians and reptiles have in common? For one thing, most of them have four legs. Only a few species have no legs at all. Scientists believe that amphibian and reptile legs developed from the muscular fins of their fish ancestors. Unlike mammals, which have their legs tucked beneath their bodies, amphibians and reptiles have legs that splay or stick out to the side.

Snakes, of course, have no legs, but can you think of any other legless amphibians and reptiles? One little-known legless amphibian is the caecilian. It is the only amphibian that is completely legless. On the muddy ground, this wormlike creature moves like a snake. But most caecilians live in the water or in wet underground tunnels. Legs would just get in the way.

Besides snakes, a few other reptiles are also legless. A glass lizard, for instance, lives in prairie grasslands, where it does not really need legs to get about. It moves along by making a swim-ming motion through the grass.

LOOK MA, NO LEGS!

The so-called "slow worm" is really a leg-less lizard. It lives in many parts of Europe, even in large cities.

Although it does not have legs, if you could look at its skeleton, you would see its leg stumps. They are all that is left of the legs its ancestors once had long ago.

Scientists believe that the ancestors of legless amphibians and reptiles, including snakes, once had legs. Many of the creatures that adopted an aquatic or burrowing life gradually lost their unnecessary limbs over the years. Snakes evolved special scales on their undersides that help them grip the ground as they slither along on their bellies. Bending their bodies swiftly back and forth and gripping with their scales, snakes can move swiftly along. They are faster without legs than with them.

Most salamanders still have four legs. Usually, they have four soft toes on their front feet and five on their back feet. But their toes can come in different arrangements depending on the species.

All salamanders, even ones that spend most of their time on land, are fast, graceful swimmers. They use their tails like

Snakes glide along using the special scales on their bellies.

paddles and tuck their legs close to their body. This makes them streamlined in the water. On land, however, salamanders are awkward. Their stubby legs bend out to the side, and they are barely long enough to raise their belly from the ground. When salamanders walk, they wiggle forward by flexing their bodies back and forth.

DID YOU KNOW?
If a salamander loses one of its legs, it can just grow another.

This cave salamander has lost its left front leg. A new one is forming.

Some aquatic salamanders have tiny limbs. The Congo "eel," which spends its life in the water, has such small feet that you might not spot them. It moves about by swimming like an eel. Another aquatic salamander, the siren, has very small front legs and no back legs at all. Mostly, it wriggles eel-like through the water. During a rainstorm, though, it can make its way overland, "swimming" through the wet grass, until it reaches another pond.

Frogs and toads are adapted for leaping. Their ankle bones are very long. They form a third section on their powerful back legs. With their long, muscled legs, frogs and toads are excellent jumpers, especially frogs. Sometimes people have contests to see which frog can leap the

A green frog is a champion leaper.

farthest. The best jumper ever recorded was a South African sharp-nosed frog. This 2-inch (5.5-centimeter) frog once made a triple leap of 33 feet 5½ inches (10 meters). Imagine how far you could leap if you had legs that strong!

Frogs are also excellent swimmers. Webbing between their long toes makes their feet into big flippers. When they stroke with their powerful back feet, they can swim amazingly fast to escape their many predators.

Some frogs and toads have other special adaptations on their feet. Some frogs have horny *tubercles* on the undersides, which protect the feet from rough surfaces and help the frogs grip the ground better. Toads have one or two large tubercles on their hind feet, which they use to dig backward into the soil.

The Surinam toad, which looks like a square pancake

with legs at the corners, has a unique adaptation of its own. Star-shaped pads on its fingertips help it probe for food in the mud. When the toad finds something, it grabs the food with its front feet and stuffs it into its mouth.

Hylid tree frogs, which spend their lives in trees, have special sticky tips on their fingers and toes, which act like suction cups. With these sticky toes, they can climb up a pane of glass. Another kind of tree frog has hands similar to ours. Its first finger acts like a thumb to the other three, so that it can grasp twigs and stems with its hands.

Wallace's flying frog has huge webbed feet. When it senses danger, it leaps from its branch, spreads its feet

The sensitive pads on the tips of a Surinam toad's fingers help it find food.

and parachutes to another tree. Its paddle-like feet help slow its fall and also help it steer. This small frog can plunge as far as 100 feet (30 meters) before landing with a plop.

All turtles and tortoises have four strong limbs. Even the heaviest land turtle can lift its body off the ground when it walks around. You can tell a lot about a turtle's habitat and behavior just by looking at its feet.

Freshwater turtles have webbed feet with claws on each of their toes. The webbing helps them swim quickly underwater, while the claws help them hold on to slippery surfaces.

Tortoises, which live entirely on land, have quite different feet. Their toes have grown together to form

A tortoise has big stump-like feet that hold up its heavy body.

solid feet, which look a lot like an elephant's. Tortoises stump about slowly, but they don't need to move fast. If a predator threatens them, they can just pull their legs and head back into their heavy, solid shells.

DIGGING IN
To escape from the desert heat, tortoises use their strong legs and tough nails to dig cool burrows in the earth.

Sea turtles spend almost all their time in the ocean. Their toes have fused or joined together to form paddle-shaped limbs that help them swim through the water. Unlike other turtles, a sea turtle's front limbs are stronger than its back limbs. Mostly, sea turtles swim with their front legs and steer with their back ones. Sea turtles are fast swimmers, but they are awkward on land. When a female comes onto a beach to lay her eggs, she has to drag her heavy body across the sand. As she pushes and pulls herself along, she leaves a distinct track—the wide trench from her body with little dents along the sides made by her paddle feet.

At first glance, lizards look a lot like salamanders, with their four, out-turned legs. But lizards have claws on their toes. Their legs, like the rest of their body, are covered with scales. Many lizards live in hot dry deserts, and their scaly bodies keep them from drying out.

A sandfish, which is not a fish at all but a lizard, lives in desert regions. Its legs are short, but it does not use

FRINGE BENEFITS

A sandfish has special fringes on its stubby feet that help it burrow into the sand to escape the desert heat.

A sandfish's short legs are not much good for walking.

them for traveling much. Instead, it "swims" through the sand like a fish.

Some lizards live around water. One of the strangest is the basilisk, which can actually run on its back limbs across the surface of the water. How does it do that? There is a fringe of scales on a basilisk's toes. When the lizard is standing still, the fringe folds over its toes, but when it runs across the water, the surface of the water forces the fringe upward. The expanded fringe increases the surface area of the foot. When a basilisk is startled, it races on its hind feet to the water and keeps on running. Thanks to its high speed and the fringes on its feet, it can dash quite a distance before it sinks. The confused predator has just lost a meal.

Other lizards are adapted to climbing on rocks.

Many geckos, for instance, have sticky pads on their toes that act like suction cups when they clamber about. They can even walk up a vertical wall.

Several other kinds of lizards have feet adapted for life in the trees. Chameleons, for example, have especially strong toes that allow them to grasp a limb firmly.

Some kinds of lizards can actually parachute from one tree to another. One kind, the flying gecko, has fleshy flaps along the sides of its body, tail, and webbed toes. When it is startled, it launches out of its tree to escape. The flaps and webbed feet slow its fall like a parachute. Another parachuting lizard, called the gliding lacertid, has a different way of slowing its fall. It has fringed scales on its toes and along the sides of its tail

A chameleon's strong toes help it grasp onto a limb.

Crocodiles have strong legs with sharp claws for digging.

that help it float safely from one tree to the next. Both these lizards can parachute about 33 feet (10 meters)—not very far, but enough to escape a hungry snake.

Alligators and crocodiles are known for their strong legs, but they don't use them for swimming. In the water, they lash or swing their heavy tails to move about. On land, alligators and crocodiles usually lie down with their legs splayed or sticking out. But these reptiles can also walk along with their heavy bodies lifted high on their powerful legs. Alligators and crocodiles cannot run very fast in that position, though. If one is in a hurry, it splays its legs out and slides along on its belly, pushing with its feet.

Most of the time, crocodiles and alligators do not move very fast. But if they are hungry and an animal comes near, they can move with great speed, lunging at their prey with their mouths gaping wide. One crocodile in particular, the Johnson's crocodile, can move especially fast. When one is startled, it gallops full speed toward the safety of the water. It moves so quickly that sometimes all four of its feet are in the air at the same time!

This emperor penguin uses its feet to cradle its chick.

BIRD FEET AND WINGS

Birds live in many different habitats so they have developed a variety of feet and legs. All birds have legs positioned directly beneath their bodies, not sticking out to the side like reptile legs. Of all the reptiles, only the dinosaurs had bird-like hips, with their legs tucked under their bodies. In fact, many scientists believe that birds descended or came from these bird-hipped reptiles. That would mean that dinosaurs are not really extinct, after all. They are simply flying around in feathered form.

Birds that spend most of their time swimming have large paddle-like feet with webbing between the toes. Many of them, including ducks and loons, have their feet set toward the back of their bodies. This gives them added power as they paddle. But it also makes them awkward on land. Waterfowl that spend more time on land, such as geese, have their legs centered under their body.

Webbed feet help to make the blue-footed booby a strong swimmer.

This means that they can walk about in fields, gathering grain, without waddling like ducks.

Besides waterfowl, there are other birds that spend a lot of time swimming or diving. Brown pelicans fly slowly over the water, peering down in search of fish. When a pelican spots its prey, it turns suddenly and dives straight down. Then it bobs back up holding a fish in its pouch. For a while after it swallows, it swims about on the surface. Its webbed toes make it a fine swimmer.

Cormorants spend a lot of time swimming with just their heads out of water. Every so often, they dive and race after fish they have spotted below. With their webbed feet set well back on their body, they are excellent swimmers and hunters.

Herons, ibises, spoonbills, and other wading birds have legs and feet adapted to different uses.

A heron's long legs allow it to wade without getting its feathers wet.

28

WALKING ON WATER?

Did you know that there is a bird that can walk on floating lily pads? The jacana, which is sometimes called the lily trotter, has incredibly long toes and claws. Those long toes spread its weight evenly so that it can walk about on floating plants. Jacanas are also aggressive birds that defend their territory fiercely. Many species have sharp spurs on their feet that they use to fight off rivals.

With their extra-long legs, these birds can wade about in the water hunting for prey without ever getting their feathers wet. They have no webbing between their toes. That would just bog them down as they step through the water. Instead, wading birds have long toes that help spread their weight out so they do not sink in the sand.

Other birds such as turkeys, grouse, and quail spend much of their time on the ground scratching for insects and other food in the soil. These birds all have short, thick legs and large sharp-clawed toes. Their feet are well adapted to walking and scratching.

One look at a hawk's feet, and you know it is a bird of prey. Hawks, eagles, falcons, ospreys, and other *raptors* all have strong legs and heavy, sharp talons. A hawk can swoop down, catch a mouse in its strong talons, then carry the meal to a nearby branch to eat it. Osprey feet are specially adapted to catching fish. On the bottoms are sharp spikes that help an osprey hold on to a slippery fish as the bird flies to its perch.

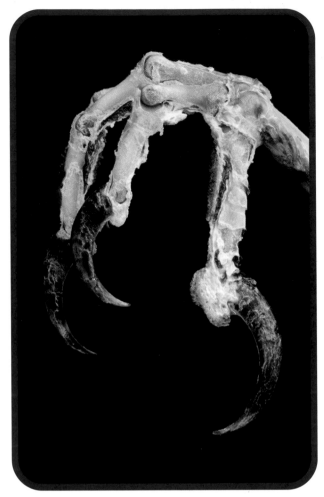

A red-tailed hawk has powerful sharp talons.

Like hawks and eagles, owls are hunters that have huge talons. An owl also has feathers on its legs and feet. Along with the soft feathers on its wings and body, an owl's leg and feet feathers muffle the sound of it swooping down on its prey.

Some birds—the swifts—look as though they have no feet at all. In fact, the name for birds in this group is *apodiformes*, which means "footless forms." Swifts spend most of their time in the air.

Since people hardly ever saw them land, they thought these birds had no feet. Of course, swifts do have feet. When they come to rest, they cling upright to a wall or a tree trunk.

UP IN THE AIR
Swifts rarely land except to nest and roost. They eat, bathe, drink, and even mate while flying.

Woodpeckers' feet are different from most other birds'. Instead of the usual arrangement, with three toes in front and one in back, woodpeckers have *zygodactyl feet*. Two toes point forward, and two point backward. This allows woodpeckers to cling to a tree trunk as they drill under the bark in search of insects.

Songbirds, including chickadees, titmice, and robins, all have feet that are especially adapted for perching. Their long back toes, which are as long as their front middle toes, help them grip firmly onto thin branches. To help matters, when a bird settles on its perch, the muscles in its feet tighten. That way, a songbird never falls off its perch, even when it is fast asleep.

Over millions of years, birds' forelegs evolved into wings. Even birds that cannot fly have wings. The special shape of the wings and feathers is what makes it possible for birds to fly.

If you look at a wing from the side, you will

A woodpecker's zygodactyl feet help it climb up tree trunks.

see that the top is more curved than the bottom. You will also notice that the wing is thicker at the front and tapers or gets slimmer toward the back. Each wing is an *airfoil*, just like an airplane wing.

How does an airfoil work? The curve of the wing forces air to travel farther over the top than across the bottom. However, the air flowing over the top reaches the back of the wing at the same time as air moving under the wing. So the air travels faster over the top. That means there is less air pressure above the wing than below, and that creates lift. Each individual flight feather is shaped the same way, and each one is its own tiny airfoil.

Birds may use their wings to escape predators or, like this barn owl, to chase after prey.

A penguin is awkward on land, but it can sail through the water up to 14 miles (24 kilometers) per hour.

To land, a bird adjusts or moves its feathers to create drag. This slows the bird and allows it to coast to its perch.

Being able to fly means that birds can escape predators. It also means birds can fly from food source to food source and migrate or travel long distances. Most birds are well adapted for flight. They have light beaks instead of heavy jaws, and their bones are filled with pockets of air. They also have powerful pectoral muscles attached to a large keel on their breastbone. The keel acts as an anchor for the strong muscles that allow a bird to fly.

Birds have different kinds of wings that suit their life in the skies. Hawks, for instance, have large, broad wings that create extra lift. These birds can glide great distances and stay soaring without having to flap their wings. Some birds, such as grouse, have small wings when compared to their body weight. To stay in the air, they have to flap their wings rapidly and constantly. All that flapping is tiring. Grouse spend most of the time pecking about on the ground. Penguins, which mostly dive for fish, have wings that have changed over time into flippers. They flap them to "fly" swiftly underwater.

Other birds, such as the well-named swifts, have long, narrow wings. With their sleek, compact wings, these birds can fly very fast. Hummingbirds, which are

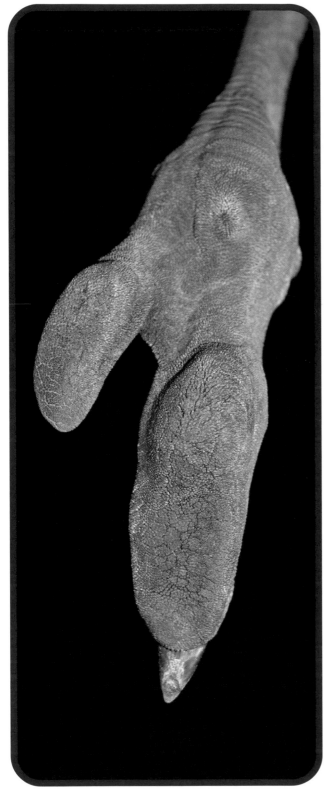

A view of the bottom of an ostrich's foot.

related to swifts, have a flying style that is all their own. They move their wings rapidly in figure eights. They can hover, and fly forward, sideways, backward, up, and down. These tiny birds can fly up to 60 miles (96 kilometers) per hour.

Some birds, of course, have lost the ability to fly. Ostriches, emus, rheas, and kiwis are all flightless. They still have wings, although they are usually small. Kiwis, small birds from New Zealand, have only tiny traces of what once were wings hidden under their shaggy feathers.

Although it may not seem so, there are advantages to being flightless. Flying takes a lot of energy and requires well-developed pectoral muscles. Flightless birds evolved in places where they had few natural predators or had other ways to flee or fight predators. Some of these birds—kiwis in particular—are at risk now because people have introduced new predators, including dogs and cats, to their formerly safe habitats.

Large flightless birds make up for not being able to fly by having long, powerful legs. The birds run swiftly on the tips of their toes. An ostrich, for example, runs on its two toes up to 45 miles (72 kilometers) per hour. That's even faster than a lion.

Ostriches can run at great speeds.

Hyenas use their sturdy claws to dig dens.

5

MAMMALS ON THE MOVE

Mammal feet and legs come in all shapes and sizes, perfectly suited to a variety of creatures that need to climb, run, and dig. You can tell a lot about a mammal's habits just by looking at its feet and legs.

All of the world's cats, including lions, bobcats, leopards, tigers, and cheetahs, are land predators. They chase down their prey using their powerful legs, then grab it with their strong, sharp claws. Most cats have *retractile* claws, which means that cats can push out their claws to grab prey or pull them in so the sharp claws are no longer dangerous or in the way. All cats can run very fast. The cheetah, in particular, has especially long legs and can sprint up to 70 miles (113 kilometers) per hour. It is the fastest mammal on earth.

Other land predators, such as wolves, coyotes, and hyenas, also have strong claws, but they are not retractile. These long-legged predators run down their prey

A SWIFT ANTELOPE
The American pronghorn is the fastest antelope. It can run up to 60 miles (95 kilometers) per hour.

and grab it in their mouths. They use their claws to dig dens where they raise their young. All land predators have tough pads on the bottoms of their feet that cushion and protect their feet as they run.

Mammals that are not predators and that live in grasslands or forests usually escape by running away on their long legs. Antelope, deer, and gazelles run on toes that have developed into two-pronged hooves. They are all swift runners.

Horses and zebras have hooves with just one toe, and they are nearly as fast as antelope. A thoroughbred horse can run up to 42 miles (67 kilometers) per hour. Even though a cheetah can run faster than these animals, it can keep up its speed only for short spurts. With a good head start, its prey can usually outrun a cheetah over time.

Other mammals escape by jumping away on their extra-long strong back legs. A jerboa, for instance, is only 6 inches tall (15 centimeters), but it can jump 10 feet (3 meters) in a single bound. A hare wallaby is no bigger than a rabbit, but it can leap higher than a person's head. Red

With their long, strong legs, red kanga-roos can hop at great speeds.

kangaroos are the champion bounders. They can grow up to 6 feet (2 meters) tall and cover 25 feet (75 meters) in a single jump with their huge hind legs. The females are faster than the males, but the males have stronger forelegs. If kangaroos are cornered, they punch with their forelegs or grab their attacker and kick with their heavily clawed hind legs.

Many mammals burrow and dig. Aardvarks, armadillos, and anteaters all have strong front legs with thick

Giant anteaters have long, sharp claws that are excellent for digging into termite nests.

sturdy claws. They use these powerful tools to dig into the hard-packed earth of termite mounds. Badgers have huge front paws equipped with long, strong claws. They use these paws to dig gophers and ground squirrels out of their burrows. Moles spend their whole lives digging underground tunnels in search of earthworms and other prey. Their shovel-like feet, with their strong, thick claws, seem to grow right out of their powerful shoulders. A mole digs so fast that it looks as if it is swimming through the earth.

Some mammals are specially adapted to climbing on rocks. A mountain goat has two hoofed toes that it

A mountain goat has rough pads on its hooves that give it a good grip.

SURE-FOOTED CHAMOIS

A chamois can balance on a small knob of rock, then leap across a 20-foot (6-meter) ravine and make a perfect landing.

spreads wide when moving over steep rocks. Rough pads on the bottom of its feet help it get a good grip. Bighorn sheep also have two spread-out toes on their rough-bottomed hooves. The hard outer edges of their hooves help keep them from slipping as they leap from rock to rock.

Other mammals have developed different kinds of legs and feet that suit a life in the trees. Gibbons, for instance, have long, strong arms twice the length of their bodies. They also have long fingers and short thumbs. When a gibbon swings from branch to branch with its long arms, it uses its fingers like hooks. But its thumbs are tucked out of the way. An opossum has sharp claws that hook into bark as it climbs about. Its big toes are separate from its other toes—sort of like our thumbs— which makes it easier to grasp branches. Squirrels have powerful hind legs that help them leap long distances from branch to branch. Squirrels can also run headfirst down a tree trunk because they can turn their clawed hind feet so they face backward.

Sloths are also well adapted to life in the trees. They hang from the branches with their long hook-like claws on the ends of their very long arms. On the ground, though, a sloth is the slowest mammal on earth. Its long

A sloth's long claws help it hold on to tree branches.

claws make it impossible to stand, and its legs are too weak to support its weight. To move along the ground, a sloth lies on its stomach and reaches forward for a place to grab hold of, then drags its body forward. Slowly, it inches itself toward the safety of a tree.

A few mammals can fly or glide to find food or to escape danger. A bat has tough membranes between its long toes that make its front feet into wings. It is the only mammal that can actually flap its wings and fly. Other mammals, including flying squirrels, flying lemurs, and sugar gliders, can sail from tree to tree. They have thin flaps of skin stretching from their wrists to their ankles. The champion glider, the sugar glider, can travel as far as 150 feet (46 meters) in a single trip. That is half the length of a football field.

Other mammals have feet adapted to walking in heavy snow. A lynx, for instance, has fur on the bottom of its large feet. When it spreads its furry toes wide, it can use them to trudge through the snow. Snowshoe hares have big snowshoe-like back feet that keep them from sinking into the snow. Polar bears have huge fur-covered paws that let them get traction on packed snow and ice. Moose have large, split hooves that help them wade through the snow. Musk oxen have curved hooves with sharp rims and soft pads. Using these hooves, they can paw through the snow to find food and climb over icy, rocky slopes.

Mammals that spend most of their time in the water have feet specially

A lynx can use its large, furry feet like snowshoes.

adapted for swimming. Beavers, muskrats, and otters all have webbed feet that act like paddles.

Other aquatic mammals have flippers instead of legs. Seals, walruses, and sea lions, for instance, have four flippers they use to dive and swim. These animals are graceful swimmers, but awkward on land.

A fur seal's front flippers are perfect for swimming.

Still other aquatic mammals have flippers in the front but no back legs. Dugongs and manatees swim about by pushing with their tails and steering with their flippers. Porpoises and whales, also, have sleek bodies with front flippers and no back legs. Like dugongs and manatees, they swim by moving their tail fin, or fluke, up and down and steering with their flippers.

THE ADAPTABLE PLATYPUS

A platypus has webbed paddle-shaped feet that help it swim swiftly through the water. Those webbed feet are also well suited to moving about on land. When a platypus climbs out of the water, the webbing folds back and out of the way. Then the platypus can run about more easily and dig with its thick nails. A male platypus has sharp venom-filled spurs on its hind legs that it uses to defend itself from predators.

Some whales are enormous and look too big to be able to move very fast. Yet a sei whale, the fastest of them all, can race along at up to 23 miles (37 kilometers) per hour. Whales and porpoises can be quite acrobatic in the water. They can turn, twirl, leap, and even swim upside down.

The more you look at all kinds of feet, the more you marvel at the different ways animals get around. What amazing adaptations animals have!

GLOSSARY

adaptation—A change in an organism that makes it more fit to survive in its environment.

airfoil—A specially shaped structure, such as a bird's wing, that provides lift in the air.

anal fin—A single fin on a fish's belly near the caudal fin.

apodiformes—The name for the natural order that includes hummingbirds and swifts.

aquatic—Living in or related to water.

caudal fin—A fish's tail fin, which helps move it forward.

dorsal fin—A fin on a fish's back that helps it to steer.

opposable thumb—A finger that is separate from the other fingers and that allows an animal to grasp objects.

order—A group of related creatures within the natural division known as a class that all share some of the same characteristics.

pectoral fins—A pair of fins behind a fish's head used for paddling and turning.

pelvic fins—A pair of fins on a fish's belly.

raptor—A bird of prey.

retractile claw—A claw such as a cat's that can be pulled back into the paw.

tubercle—The name for the horny knobs on the bottom of a frog or toad's foot.

vertebra—One of the bony segments that make up the spinal column.

zygodactyl feet—Feet with two toes pointed forward and two toes pointing backward.

FIND OUT MORE

BOOKS

Barre, Michel. *Animal Senses*. Milwaukee, WI: Gareth Stevens, 1998.

Berger, Melvin. *Flies Taste with Their Feet: Weird Facts about Insects*. Minneapolis, MN: Econo-Clad Books, 1999.

Cerfolli, Fulvio. *Adapting to the Environment*. Austin, TX: Raintree Steck-Vaughn, 1999.

Grambo, Rebecca L. *Claws and Jaws*. Vero Beach, FL: Rourke, 2002.

Hickman, Pamela, and Pat Stephens. *Animal Senses: How Animals See, Hear, Taste, Smell, and Feel*. Buffalo, NY: Kids Can Press, 1998.

Kalman, Bobbie. *How Do Animals Adapt?* New York: Crabtree Publishing, 2000.

Parker, Steve. *Adaptation*. Chicago, IL: Heinemann Library, 2001.

Viegas, Jennifer. *The Lower Limbs: Learning How We Use Our Thighs, Knees, Legs, and Feet*. New York: Rosen, 2002.

WEB SITES

The Animal Diversity Web
http://animaldiversity.ummz.umich.edu/site/index.htm
This site contains information about individual species in several different classes of animals, particularly mammals.

Audubon Society
http://www.audubon.org
This organization is an amazing source of information for people interested in birds and bird-watching.

Cyber School—Marine Life
http://ourworld.compuserve.com/Homepages/jaap/Mmlinks.htm
This site provides information on many fishes and other marine life.

Insect Inspecta World
http://www.insecta-inspecta.com
This site has all kinds of information about insects.

INDEX

Page numbers for illustrations are in **boldface.**

ABOUT THE AUTHOR

Sara Swan Miller has enjoyed working with children all her life, first as a Montessori nursery school teacher and later as an outdoor environmental educator at the Mohonk Preserve in New Paltz, New York. As director of the school program, she has taught hundreds of children the importance of appreciating the natural world.

She has written more than fifty books, including *Three Stories You Can Read to Your Dog; Three Stories You Can Read to Your Cat; Three More Stories You Can Read to Your Dog; Three More Stories You Can Read to Your Cat; Three Stories You Can Read to Your Teddy Bear; Will You Sting Me? Will You Bite? The Truth About Some Scary-Looking Insects;* and *What's in the Woods? An Outdoor Activity Book.* She has also written many nonfiction books for children.